A scene from the Westport Country Playhouse production of "The Fourth Wall." Set design by Richard Ellis.

THE
FOURTH
WALL

BY A.R. Gurney

★

★

DRAMATISTS
PLAY SERVICE
INC.

To David Saint

THE FOURTH WALL was first produced at Westport Country Playhouse (James B. McKenzie, Executive Director; Eric Friedheim, Associate Producer), in Westport, Connecticut, opening on August, 3, 1992, continuing on to the Cape Playhouse, in Dennis, Massachusetts, on August 17, 1992, and then to the Hasty Pudding Theater, in Cambridge, Massachusetts, in September, 1992 (Andreas Teuber, Producer). It was directed by David Saint; the set design was by Richard Ellis; the costume design was by David Murin; the lighting design was by Susan Roth; the Cole Porter songs used were arranged by Jonathan Sheffer and the stage manager was Ira Mont. The cast was as follows:

ROGER.. Tony Roberts
JULIA .... Kelly Bishop
PEGGY.. E. Katherine Kerr
FLOYD .... Jack Gilpin

THE FOURTH WALL was subsequently produced by Norman Rubenstein's Feenix Productions, in conjunction with James B. McKenzie and Ralph Roseman, at the Briar Street Theatre in Chicago, Illinois, in April, 1993. The set design was by Richard Ellis; the costume design was by Gayland Spaulding; the lighting design was by J.R. Lederle and the production stage manager was Rebecca Green. The director was again David Saint. The cast was as follows:

ROGER .... George Segal
JULIA .... Jean de Baer
PEGGY .... Betty Buckley
FLOYD .... Mark Nelson

THE FOURTH WALL most recent professional production was at the Pasadena Playhouse, in Pasadena, California, opening on March 20, 1994, and continuing on to the Poway Center for the Performing Arts in San Diego, California. The set design was by Scott Heineman; the costume design was by Zoe DuFour; the lighting design was by Martin Aronstein; musical arrangement was by Ron Abel and the production stage manager was Daniel Munson. David Saint once again directed. The cast was as follows:

ROGER .... Sam Freed
JULIA .... Jean de Baer
PEGGY .... Barrie Youngfellow
FLOYD .... Jim Fyfe

CAST
(in order of appearance)

JULIA
ROGER
PEGGY
FLOYD

The first three are middle-aged. Floyd is somewhat younger.

The living room of a suburban house near Buffalo. It looks pleasant, comfortable and lived-in. Upstage is an inviting fireplace. Upstage, too, a baby grand piano, its keyboard toward the wall. Also upstage, a picture window, through which one can see the pleasant greenery of a suburban backyard. Downstage, there are a couch, chairs, and tables, all somewhat artificially placed to face front. Down right, a working bar. Down left, a telephone, below the entrance to a front hall. On the walls are several good, rather conventional paintings, On the piano, a number of family photographs. On the mantelpiece, several knick-knacks.

(NOTE: this description applies to a proscenium theatre. I hope a good designer could attain a similar effect on a more open stage.)

The time is the present, beginning in late afternoon and continuing on into the evening.

THE FOURTH WALL

ACT ONE

At rise, there is no one onstage. Through the windows comes late afternoon light. After a moment, Roger and Julia enter from the hall. Roger wears a business suit. Julia wears the latest thing in New York fashion.

ROGER. *(Indicating the proscenium "wall.")* You see?

JULIA. I do.

ROGER. I thought you should see.

JULIA. I certainly do. *(She looks at the "wall" carefully.)*

ROGER. This wall …

JULIA. Yes, this blank wall. *(She looks around.)* The other walls are quite attractive.

ROGER. I agree.

JULIA. I like the looks of these other walls.

ROGER. Thank you very much.

JULIA. *(Returning to the proscenium.)* It's just — this one.

ROGER. This fourth one.

JULIA. This is the one that throws me for a loop.

ROGER. I figured it might.

JULIA. I mean, it's just — there, Roger. This great, blank, undecorated — wall.

ROGER. I thought you should see it first-hand.

JULIA. Yes. I'm glad I flew up. Otherwise I wouldn't have believed it. *(She ponders it.)*

ROGER. Now Julia, living in New York, you must be familiar with a variety of private residences.

JULIA. Too familiar, according to my last husband.

ROGER. Well I imagine they've been decorated in many different ways.

JULIA. You'd be amazed what New Yorkers do to adorn

7

their dens. It's their way of warding off evil.

ROGER.   All right, then. Tell me frankly: Have you ever, in all your experience, seen a room done quite like this?

JULIA.   You mean, with this ... wall?

ROGER.   With this wall.

JULIA.   Only.... But no.

ROGER.   You were going to say?

JULIA.   Roger. Do you remember those plays that used to begin with an attractive woman and a charming man coming in and talking?

ROGER.   I do.

JULIA.   This reminds me of those rooms they talked in.

ROGER.   All right. Now keep that thought in mind, and tell me something else. Do you like it?

JULIA.   This wall?

ROGER.   This wall.

JULIA.   Roger, I've been in New York long enough never to pass judgment on how people live. We have the *New York Times* to do that.

ROGER.   No, now come on, Julia. We grew up together here in Buffalo. I remember once, in third grade, you took me aside and told me you could see my underpants.

JULIA.   Did I do that?

ROGER.   You did. And I corrected the problem immediately. It saved me considerable embarrassment during recess.

JULIA.   All right. Then I'll speak out again. Do I like this room? No, I do not. But maybe it's just how things are placed.

ROGER.   Placed?

JULIA.   The furniture. I mean, if this wall were behind you, you might be able to live with it. You could ignore it. Or simply glance at it occasionally. Over your shoulder. Like this. *(She demonstrates.)* See? It could be a kind of conversation piece. But with your furniture facing it, you're forced to confront it, almost head on, whenever you're in the room.

ROGER.   That's the thing, isn't it.

JULIA.   That's the thing. I'll go one step farther, Roger. Your decorator should be shot at sunrise.

ROGER.   No decorator is responsible for this wall, Julia.

JULIA.   No decorator? Then who?

ROGER.   Peggy.

JULIA.   Peggy? Your wife Peggy? My old friend Peggy? Who was known in the past for her quiet, good taste?

ROGER.   This is the way she wants this room.

JULIA.   But is she serious?

ROGER.   She's never been more serious in her life.

JULIA.   But what if you proved to her that she's made a serious mistake? What, for example, if you took this couch, and unobtrusively eased it around to face that cozy fireplace?

ROGER.   Peggy would unobtrusively ease it right back.

JULIA.   And if you focused things on that pleasant greenery?

ROGER.   Peggy would *re*focus them, the first chance she got.

JULIA.   To face that blank wall?

ROGER.   To face that blank wall.

JULIA.   But why is Peggy behaving so strangely?

ROGER.   I wish I knew.

JULIA.   I keep thinking of plays.

ROGER.   I asked you to keep them in mind.

JULIA.   Doesn't this room make you feel, the minute you walk in, as if you were *acting* in one?

ROGER.   It does, Julia! And perhaps you've noticed, since we've been here, we've begun to talk in an artificial and stagey sort of way.

JULIA.   I *have* noticed that! And it's hard work! I mean, not only do I have to think about what to say, but I have to think how best to say it!

ROGER.   Me, too!... I mean, I also.

JULIA.   It's exhausting, Roger.

ROGER.   Of course it is. And remember, you're just a visitor. This is my living room. I have to live here.

JULIA.   But couldn't you retreat to another room? There must be a den somewhere.

ROGER.   I escape to it when I can. But Peggy keeps coming in here, and since I like being with her, I follow along. And that's when the trouble starts.

JULIA.   Trouble?

ROGER.   The minute we get in here, she becomes restless and impatient. And I feel obligated to keep her interested. The result is, more and more, I find myself performing like a trained seal in front of this goddamn *wall*, trying to ignore it, trying *not* to ignore it, constantly aware that I'm very much on the line as a husband, as a man, and as an actor.

JULIA.   Have you had any stage experience?

ROGER.   None at all! I'm a businessman, Julia! I run a small factory here in Buffalo. We manufacture spherical distributors.

JULIA.   Spherical distributors.... Now don't tell me. They go in the engines of automobiles.

ROGER.   No, no. They're those plastic balls that go in roll-on deodorants.

JULIA.   How post-industrial! I imagine, in these anxious times, you're doing very well.

ROGER.   Success means nothing, Julia, when, at the end of the day, I'm forced to confront this great blank wall. Have you ever read Melville's *Bartleby*?

JULIA.   Of course not.

ROGER.   Well I have. It's about — Oh hell. Skip it. Have a drink, Julia.

JULIA.   Oh I don't know. No one drinks much in New York any more. At least in public.

ROGER.   Just a glass of champagne?

JULIA.   *(Looks at her watch.)* Actually, I should catch a plane back. I'm meeting someone tonight for some safe sex. *(She starts out.)* I'll send you a bill for my consulting fee.

ROGER.   Don't go, Julia. Please. It's hell being left alone in this room. You feel compelled to have something to do.

JULIA.   It's also a hard room to leave. I keep thinking I need a better exit line.

ROGER.   Then have some champagne as an excuse to stay.

JULIA.   All right. Just a glass. For old time's sake.

ROGER.   Good. *(He goes to the bar, gets out a bottle of champagne and two glasses. Julia sits self-consciously on the couch.)*

JULIA.   I must say, I am amazed by what I've seen, Roger. From the looks of your annual Christmas card, I would have said that Peggy was primarily interested in children and dogs.

ROGER.   She used to be. She also had a strong commitment to community service. It was only after our last child went off to college, and our Dalmatian died, and the funds for the downtown community center dried up, that she started rearranging our furniture. *(He pops the champagne and pours.)* But welcome back to Buffalo. *(They clink glasses and drink.)* Do you like this champagne, by the way?

JULIA.   May I be frank again?

ROGER.   I wish you would be.

JULIA.   Then no, I don't.

ROGER.   That's because it's *stage* champagne, Julia! It's basically ginger-ale. I don't dare serve alcoholic beverages in this room, for fear we'll slur our words, or say something stupid in front of that goddamn fourth wall! *(Peggy's voice is heard off off-stage.)*

PEGGY'S VOICE.   Hello!

ROGER.   But there's Peggy now. You should see for yourself. *(Calls off.)* We're in here, darling.

JULIA.   Quickly. How should I behave?

ROGER.   Try to be natural.

JULIA.   I can't! I haven't been natural in years! I'll be theatrical. The situation seems to call for it. *(Peggy comes in. She wears simple, comfortable clothes.)*

PEGGY.   *(To Roger.)* Hello, dear. *(Kisses Roger.)*

ROGER.   Look who flew up from New York, darling. Our old friend Julia.

JULIA.   *(Dramatically; holding out her arms in greeting.)* Peggy!

PEGGY.   Why, Julia! Hello! *(They kiss.)*

JULIA.   It's both cheeks in New York, darling. Like alternate parking. *(Peggy kisses the other cheek.)*

ROGER.   Where've you been, dear?

PEGGY.   Oh, out and around.

JULIA.   I hear you're a do-gooder, Peggy. Have you been helping the homeless and stuff?

PEGGY.   I wish I could. *(She sits and looks at the wall.)* Have you noticed my wall?

JULIA.   I have to admit the subject came up, Peggy.

11

PEGGY.   What does it do to you?

JULIA.   Well, Peggy, it — raises a number of fascinating questions.

ROGER.   I've been trying to answer them, darling.

JULIA.   In the theatre I think they call it exposition.

PEGGY.   Is that where they go over old ground?

JULIA.   Exactly, Peggy!

PEGGY.   *(Getting up.)* There's too much exposition in the world! *(She starts out.)* I have to make a telephone call.

ROGER.   Who to, dear?

PEGGY.   Oh I'll think of someone. *(She exits. Pause.)*

ROGER.   We lost her.

JULIA.   I'm furious, Roger. She treated me as if I were simply an extra! We hardly made eye contact!

ROGER.   She does it a lot.

JULIA.   But we grew up together, I haven't seen her in years, and now she trumps up an excuse to walk off!

ROGER.   Don't take it personally, Julia. The other night I organized a small dinner party, and she did the same thing.

JULIA.   Dinner party? Why didn't you invite *me*? I shine at dinner parties.

ROGER.   Oh it was just a little thing: a few folks who happened to be in town. Governor Cuomo ... Cornelius Bennett, of the Buffalo Bills ... Kitty Carlisle Hart.... That crowd.

JULIA.   I would have flown up immediately. I've been dying to sleep with all three of them.

ROGER.   When you hear what happened, you'll be glad you didn't come. Like a fool, I served everybody cocktails made with real alcohol. As a result, the conversation became somewhat random. So Peggy got impatient and left the room.

JULIA.   I hope she had a better exit line.

ROGER.   It was worse. She announced she wanted to take a bath.

JULIA.   Good Lord! Did she need one?

ROGER.   Not at all. But she spent the rest of the evening in the tub, reading *The New Republic.*

JULIA.   What did you do?

ROGER.   I tried to keep things going, but it wasn't easy, with my wife splashing around off-stage. And singing.

JULIA.   Singing what?

ROGER.   "If I had a Hammer."

JULIA.   How horrible! Something has got to be done!

ROGER.   That's why I asked you to fly up. I thought you might get a handle on all this, being a woman and a New Yorker.

JULIA.   I'm very glad I'm both. *(Pacing and thinking.)* Now let me think … I am reviewing in my mind what I have read recently in the Living Section of the *New York Times* … *(More thinking.)* Yes.... Mmmmm.... Yes.... Roger, I've got it!… This room … these strange entrances and exits … Peggy, in her middle years, has come to see her life as some sort of play.

ROGER.   You think that's it?

JULIA.   Of course! It happens a lot with suburban women. The empty nest, all that. Most of them learn to accept the situation, and settle for a supporting role.

ROGER.   But not Peggy?

JULIA.   Peggy seems to be warming up for a major part. Which is outrageous, when you think about it. I mean, she's had no New York experience.

ROGER.   But to her, we're all in some play?

JULIA.   Exactly. And apparently she wants us to act it out. I must say it might be fun, as long as we keep it regional and not-for-profit.

ROGER.   But it's not fair! I mean, here I am, rich and free, kids educated, ready to celebrate not only my own success but the success of capitalism in general, when suddenly my wife wants me to perform some unknown play in front of some stupid fourth wall!

JULIA.   Now, now.

ROGER.   But I hate it, Julia! I'm beginning to see the whole world as simply a stage, and all of us men and women simply actors strutting around on it.

JULIA.   Others have said that before, Roger. And said it better.

ROGER.   That's because I'm no good at making up *lines,*

Julia! Goddammit, it's no fair!

JULIA. Now Roger, get a hold of yourself. If Peggy wants a play, surely she must have a plot. What do you think her plot is?

ROGER. I don't know, I don't know, I don't KNOW! And I don't think she does either! I'm trying to be a good sport about things, but I'm totally unclear about what I'm supposed to be doing. *(Peggy's voice is heard off-stage.)*

PEGGY'S VOICE. I'm coming back!

ROGER. She's coming back. Tell me what to do.

JULIA. Try making a speech.

ROGER. A speech?

JULIA. Give her something to react to.

ROGER. But — *(Peggy re-enters.)*

PEGGY. Have I missed anything?

ROGER. We've missed *you,* darling.

PEGGY. What's been going on?

JULIA. Oh well. We've been drinking champagne and doing light dialogue, Peggy.

PEGGY. Is that all? I was hoping there might be more.

JULIA. I agree with you, Peggy. *(Low to Roger.)* There's your cue.

ROGER. *(Taking a deep breath.)* Peggy, darling, let me remind you of something. This is our *living* room, dear. This is where you and I have *lived* for over twenty years.

PEGGY. I know that.

ROGER. *(Indicates the pictures on the piano.)* No but see? Here is our family, dear, arranged happily on the piano.... Our children. Teddy in Little League, Elsie graduating from High School ...

JULIA. How sweet.

ROGER. And our parents, Peggy.... Mine on that trip to Italy. Yours when they came for Thanksgiving ...

PEGGY. *(To Julia.)* They fought all during dessert.

ROGER. No, but look, love. Our hearth. Our mantelpiece. Your community service award, nestled alongside my Buffalo Better Business medal ... *(Indicates a vase on the table.)* And here is the lovely vase our friends gave us ...

PEGGY. For our fifteenth anniversary ...

ROGER. Right! And there on the rug is where the dog peed.... And that spot on the wall, from when you threw your drink at Madge Baxter during the Vietnam war ...

PEGGY. She wanted to assassinate Jane Fonda.

ROGER. *(Goes to the window.)* And look out the window, sweetie. Look out in the yard. There's the sandbox I made for the kids, before the cat started using it.... And the stump which was home-plate during the whiffle-ball games ... and the maple tree, which is now as high as the house ...

JULIA. This is a lovely speech he's giving, Peggy. It's too long, but it's lovely.

PEGGY. I know it is.

ROGER. Then come on, sweetie, look this way, face this way, not at some dumb blank wall.

PEGGY. I can't.

ROGER. Why the hell NOT?

PEGGY. It's not enough.

ROGER. Not enough? Our life together has not been enough?

PEGGY. There should be more. *(She looks dreamingly at the wall.)*

JULIA. I think she wants you to get deeper, Roger.

ROGER. Deeper?

JULIA. Isn't that it, Peggy? You want it deeper.

PEGGY. Maybe ...

JULIA. *(To Roger.)* Try the speech again, but this time make it deeper. And shorter.

ROGER. O.K. ... *(Clears his throat; starts again.)* Peg, sweetheart, this is our life. Here on the piano — Goddammmit! I can't do this, Peg!

PEGGY. I know you can't.

JULIA. What we really need is a plot, Peggy.

PEGGY. Maybe that's it.

JULIA. I think it is. You don't have one up your sleeve, do you? Just to get us all going.

PEGGY. No I don't. I really don't. *(She gets up.)* But I do have the sense we're missing something. *(She goes off. Pause.)*

JULIA.   I'll tell you one thing, Roger. Those sudden exits are becoming irritating. She needs a good director.

ROGER.   Maybe if you talked to her alone ...

JULIA.   I don't think I can.

ROGER.   Now come on, Julia. I paid your fare. With what the airlines charge these days, it's the least you can do.

JULIA.   I'm just not sure I'm up to it, Roger.

ROGER.   Come on. You're a woman, after all.

JULIA.   That's exactly why I can't.

ROGER.   What do you mean?

JULIA.   Roger: Any scene I had with Peggy would be doomed to fail.

ROGER.   Why?

JULIA.   Because I want it to fail.

ROGER.   You want it to fail?

JULIA.   I suddenly find myself wanting Peggy to continue down this strange theatrical road. I also want you to become so frustrated with her that you'll turn elsewhere for solace and sex.

ROGER.   Elsewhere?

JULIA.   Namely to me.

ROGER.   Uh oh.

JULIA.   I'm sorry, but that's what I want.

ROGER.   I'm amazed, Julia.

JULIA.   So am I. But what can we do? We've got to have a plot, and this is the only one I can come up with.

ROGER.   But surely, living in New York, you have other sexual commitments. Lovers, a new husband, various lesbian affiliations ...

JULIA.   Of course! I'm supposed to be meeting one of the above this evening.

ROGER.   I remember you mentioned an appointment.

JULIA.   But now I have no intention of keeping it. I now feel feelings I haven't felt since I saw your underpants in third grade.

ROGER.   Oh hey.

JULIA.   I'm here, Roger, and I'm available, and I'm famished for love. And so it's cruel of you to ask me to play a scene which goes so much against my own sexual objectives.

ROGER.   Oh boy. This is a tough one.

JULIA.   There it is.

ROGER.   Have more champagne while we think about it.

JULIA.   Better not. Given the mood I'm in, even fake champagne might make me more aggressive.

ROGER.   So. Gosh. Wow. I mean, I fly you up to help me get my wife back, and now you say you want to become lovers.

JULIA.   At least it's a plot, Roger.

ROGER.   It is. It is definitely a plot. *(He thinks.)* Well look. I'm an amateur here — I'm perfectly willing to admit it. But it seems to me that the theatre is riddled with scenes of self-sacrifice. If you played out such a scene with Peggy, you'd be working to repair a marriage which your own sexual appetites are tempting you to destroy. I may be wrong, but I think the stuff of real drama might lie in a scene like that.

JULIA.   You think so?

ROGER.   I do. In fact, it sounds like a star turn to me. If there were critics beyond that wall, Julia, they might be convinced by that scene that you belonged above the title, and ahead of all the rest of us, even out of alphabetical order.

JULIA.   Then I'll do it.

ROGER.   *(Kissing her.)* Oh thanks, Julia.

JULIA.   You shouldn't have kissed me, Roger. It whets my sexual appetite.

ROGER.   That's why I did it.

JULIA.   You're a ruthless man.

ROGER.   I'm learning you have to be ruthless in the theatre. *(He calls off.)* I think we're getting somewhere, Peggy! *(Peggy's voice is heard off-stage.)*

PEGGY'S VOICE.   I'll be right in!

JULIA.   Does she listen off-stage?

ROGER.   Of course not.

JULIA.   Are you sure? It might affect how I play the scene.

ROGER.   My wife is no eavesdropper, Julia!

JULIA.   But she's so much on cue.

ROGER.   That's this *room* again! It makes everything seem contrived and mechanical! That's why I need your help! Now I'll duck out, so you two women can have what the French call a "tit a tit."

JULIA.   I find that remark offensive, Roger!

ROGER.   I do, too, goddammit! See? See what's happening? Now I'm going for cheap laughs which ridicule women! Oh help me, Julia. Please!

JULIA.   I'll do what I can to cope with an impossible situation. No New Yorker can do better than that. *(Peggy re-enters.)*

PEGGY.   Here I am.

ROGER.   I'll go watch the ball game in the den.

PEGGY.   You're not staying?

ROGER.   Sorry. I've been working my ass off since square one. I need some time on the bench. *(He goes off.)*

PEGGY.   *(To Julia.)* He's upset.

JULIA.   *(Going to the couch.)* That's what I want to talk to you about. *(She sits.)*

PEGGY.   Shoot.

JULIA.   *(Patting a place for Peggy on the couch.)* Peggy, dear: Normally, in New York, when we talk to our friends, and we suspect the conversation might become confrontational, we try to ease into the issue with a few pleasant preliminaries. We refer to the weather, we touch on current events, we recall moments in the past which may have been mutually agreeable. Only after these diversionary overtures have been thoroughly played out do we gingerly step across the border into the area of controversy.

PEGGY.   Sounds like a complicated way to keep friends, Julia.

JULIA.   Well it works. But in your case, the issue is so compelling I plan to rush right to the point. Peggy: What's the story on this fucking fourth wall?

PEGGY.   I wish I knew.

JULIA.   I won't accept that as an answer, Peggy.

PEGGY.   It's always been there, you know. That wall. I'm just calling attention to it.

JULIA.   But it makes people self-conscious, Peggy. It forces them to perform.

18

PEGGY.   That might be a step in the right direction.

JULIA.   WHAT direction? We have no idea where you're taking us, Peggy. With this wall.

PEGGY.   What if we could break through it, Julia?

JULIA.   Break *through* it?

PEGGY.   What if something wonderful lies beyond it?

JULIA.   I'll tell you what lies beyond it, Peggy. Your dining room lies beyond it. So if you broke through it, you'd end up in an entirely different play.

PEGGY.   What if you're wrong, Julia? What if there were people beyond that wall? What if these people had paid money to be there? What if they had given up reading a book, or watching television, or going to some game, and were now there, sitting there, waiting for us to reach them?

JULIA.   Oh now Peggy ...

PEGGY.   No, what if it were true? And what if this audience were really democratic, Julia? What if there were poor people there, as well as rich? And what if they were ethnically diverse? What, for example, if there were a decent number of African-Americans out there?

JULIA.   They'd HATE this thing, Peggy. They'd rush right off to August Wilson.

PEGGY.   But maybe they've *stayed*, Julia. And maybe Asians and Latinos are there too, and maybe they've all come hoping we'll break through, and reach them where they live.

JULIA.   *(Looking out, uneasily.)* If any people are out there at all, Peggy, I suspect they're primarily Jewish. The poor things have kept the theatre going almost single-handedly for the last thirty years.

PEGGY.   Then we should reach them, too.

JULIA.   Neil Simon already does that, dear.

PEGGY.   And we should connect to the Arab community.

JULIA.   You just blew it, dear.

PEGGY.   I don't care. And we should reach gays and lesbians and —

JULIA.   Lesbians have been mentioned, Peggy. The word definitely came up in my scene with Roger.

PEGGY.   But that wall is still there. And I'd give my eye-teeth to get beyond it.

JULIA.   Peggy darling, try to remember that walls were put on this earth for two purposes: to hold up ceilings and keep people from killing each other. I'm all for them, and so I believe are most architects.

PEGGY.   I don't agree, Julia. My entire life has been devoted to the breaching of walls. I broke through the wall between childhood and adolescence. I broke through the wall between single life and marriage. Then Roger and I built our own cozy wall around home and family, but I broke through that when I got a job. And then I only saw more walls — walls upon walls, everywhere I looked. I see a wall between you and me, Julia.

JULIA.   I hope there is, Peggy. At school, they made us memorize Robert Frost.

PEGGY.   I know, I know. "Stone walls make good neighbors." But maybe we're too hung up on these ramparts we watch. Maybe this wall — this last wall, this fourth wall — is just an illusion. All I know is I'll never be happy — never, Julia! — until I've at least *tried* to see beyond it, and get through it, and leave it behind me forever! *(Pause.)*

JULIA.   Peggy, darling. Look: I've only been here ... *(Checks her watch.)* twenty minutes, and already I feel this pressing need to take some sort of action. It's as if someone were constantly whispering in my ear, saying, "Move it, lady. Get to the plot!"

PEGGY.   I hear something else ...

JULIA.   Such as what?

PEGGY.   I don't know ... something very different.... Something calling from beyond that wall ...

JULIA.   Saying?

PEGGY.   I'm not sure.... Something like "Come on in. The water's fine."

JULIA.   I'm not interested in playing Esther Williams, Peggy. Now stop trying to be avant-garde, Peggy, and start thinking about your marriage.

PEGGY.   Did Roger talk about that?

JULIA.   I never reveal my sources.

PEGGY.   I'm hoping this wall will improve our marriage, Julia. I'm hoping one of these days, he and I will sit down in front of it and be forced to talk seriously about important things. How many married couples ever do that? How many talk at all? Most of them simply eye each other at meals, and fight when they get in the car.

JULIA.   You might lose him, Peggy.

PEGGY.   Why do you think that?

JULIA.   I sense he's being pulled in another direction.

PEGGY.   I sense that, too.

JULIA.   Then turn away from this wall, darling! And turn your furniture away from it. Stand up right now and turn your back to it!

PEGGY.   No thanks. I've been turning my back on things for too long. That wall is there, and even if there's nothing beyond it, I have to behave as if people were there.

JULIA.   Even if you don't know where you're going?

PEGGY.   Even so.

JULIA.   Even if your behavior forces your husband into the arms of another — well, I won't give away the only plot we have.

PEGGY.   I'm sorry. Here I stand.

JULIA.   Then we'll have to play things out, each in her own way.

PEGGY.   I'm afraid so.

JULIA.   It seems to me our scene is virtually over.

PEGGY.   I think it is.... And now I'd better go do something about dinner. *(Starts off; then stops.)* You're welcome to stay, by the way. We normally eat in the kitchen, and things get more cozy and informal in there.

JULIA.   I might, Peggy. It depends on what happens in my next scene.

PEGGY.   Fair enough.

JULIA.   So would you send Roger in as you pass by the den? I want to tell him something.

PEGGY.   O.K.

JULIA.   And please ask him to make it snappy. I'd hate to be stuck out here alone — doing clichéd stage business, like

21

thumbing through a magazine or fussing with my hair … I'd hate that, Peggy, fourth wall or not.

PEGGY. Why don't you play the piano?

JULIA. Because I don't know how.

PEGGY. Don't worry. It plays itself. It's one of those player pianos made by the old Wurlitzer Company, in Niagara Falls. *(She goes out.)*

JULIA. *(Calling after her.)* I'm not interested in provincial nostalgia, Peggy. I left all that behind back here in Buffalo. *(She soon is thumbing through a magazine, and combing her hair. But then she is drawn to the piano. She goes to it, stands by it, tentatively hits a key. It immediately starts to play an introduction to a song. She is surprised for a second, then listens. Then the piano plays a single note, as if sounding her key. She sings the note. Singing.)* Ah. *(To herself.)* Too high. *(The piano sounds another note. Julia tries it.)* Better. *(The piano finds her key.)* Good. *(She begins to sing along. Singing.)*

"I'm in love again,
And the spring is comin'
I'm in love again,
Hear my heart strings strummin'
I'm in love again,
And the hymn I'm hummin'
Is the "Huddle Up, Cuddle Up Blues!"

(She gets up, begins to "perform" the song as the piano continues to accompany her.)

I'm in love again,
And I can't rise above it,
I'm in love again,
And I love, love, love it:
I'm in love again,
And I'm darn glad of it,
Good news!*

(Roger enters, as the music continues under. He now wears a sweater.)

ROGER. I see you've discovered our player piano.

* See Special Note on Music on copyright page.

JULIA.   Yes.

ROGER.   I programmed it strictly for Cole Porter.

JULIA.   I noticed that. *(They now sing together.)*

BOTH.   *(Singing.)*

> "I'm in love again,
> And I love, love, love it:
> I'm in love again,
> And I'm darn glad of it,
> Good news!"*

(They end with a good finish.)

ROGER.   Well?

JULIA.   Do you think we could squeeze out one more reprise?

ROGER.   I'm concerned about Peggy. She said you had something to say.

JULIA.   Oh. Right. I do. Brace yourself, Roger. I've decided your wife is insane.

ROGER.   Oh now ...

JULIA.   Nuts. Totally. Mad as a hatter.

ROGER.   Are you sure?

JULIA.   Look, if it were just a question of play-acting in this room, I'd say, fine, let's keep it up. As you know, I'm beginning to enjoy it. But she wants to break *through*, Roger.

ROGER.   To where?

JULIA.   To some other *side*. To *reach* people. Of different *backgrounds*. I wouldn't be surprised if she wanted to *touch* them. It's the Sixties without the Beatles!

ROGER.   Good Lord.

JULIA.   And she has no PLOT, Roger! Not even a subplot. Nothing but some vague desire to make connections.

ROGER.   You make her sound like an unemployed telephone operator.

JULIA.   *(Moving toward him.)* At least I have a plot.

ROGER.   Did you tell her that?

JULIA.   I broadly hinted at it.

ROGER.   What did she say?

* See Special Note on Music on copyright page.

23

JULIA.   Nothing.

ROGER.   She didn't care?

JULIA.   All she cares about is that stupid wall. Now I've done what I can as a concerned friend of the family. It's time to ship her off to the funny farm, toot sweet.

ROGER.   Oh well gee, Julia ...

JULIA.   No, I'm serious. The poor soul needs help. Call the men in white, and get her out of here!

ROGER.   But Peggy and I have been married so long. To see her grappled to the ground, forced into a straight jacket ...

JULIA.   They did it to Blanche Du Bois in *Streetcar*. It was profoundly moving.

ROGER.   But we're talking about my wife ... the mother of my children ...

JULIA.   No, now be strong, Roger.... Stride to that telephone and dial manfully!

ROGER.   But I don't know the number of the insane asylum.

JULIA.   976-NUTS. I saw it advertised at the airport.

ROGER.   *(Jiggling the phone.)* Our phone's out of order.

JULIA.   I don't believe that.

ROGER.   *(Listening.)* One of our kids is on the extension.

JULIA.   Your children are not here, Roger. You're becoming totally implausible. Now telephone. Or I will. *(He dials reluctantly. A car door is heard slamming off-stage.)* What's that?

ROGER.   A car door slamming.

JULIA.   Don't tell me the ambulance has arrived already? That's awfully fast work, even for the theatre.

ROGER.   *(Hanging up the phone.)* This may be someone else, Julia. Peggy will let him in.

JULIA.   Let who in? You obviously know who it is.

ROGER.   I do, Julia. Sit down, and I'll try to tell you.

JULIA.   *(Sitting.)* I sense a twist that I'm unprepared for.

ROGER.   Have some champagne, Julia.

JULIA.   I've already told you, no. Now stop stalling, and tell me what's going on.

ROGER.   All right, Julia.... While you were having your scene with Peggy, I went, as I said I would, to watch the ball

24

game. When I got there, however, I found I couldn't concentrate. Not only did I find myself torn between two women, but also I felt trapped in a play not of my own making.

JULIA.   I can understand your confusion.

ROGER.   Finally, out of desperation, I made a telephone call.

JULIA.   A telephone call?

ROGER.   To the State University Department of Drama. I thought if anyone could resolve this dilemma, someone who has committed his life to the study of drama might be able to do so.

JULIA.   So you dialed SUNY-Buffalo?

ROGER.   I did. I braved their new touch-tone centrex answering system. I defied the rudeness of the students who kept putting me on hold. But finally I found myself speaking to a member of the drama faculty named Professor Loesser.

JULIA.   Professor Loesser ...

ROGER.   Naturally he prefers that we call him simply by his first name, Floyd.

JULIA.   Rather than Professor Loesser. Yes. All that makes sense.

ROGER.   I explained to him our problem, and asked him to stop by. Like most academics, he had nothing else to do. I strongly suspect, therefore, that this now may be Floyd, arriving at our front door. (*Door chimes are heard off-stage. Roger calls off.*) Would you get the door, darling?

JULIA.   I must say, Roger, I'm a little hurt. You ask for my advice, and now you're suddenly calling in a second opinion.

ROGER.   I had to, Julia. We need the cool, dispassionate eye of academia to examine our situation and advise what steps to take next.

JULIA.   I've never much liked university professors. I've had affairs with several, and they all seem obsessed with tenure.... No, no. I'm worried about this Floyd person already. (*Peggy comes in with Floyd, who is younger, wears jeans and a corduroy jacket, and carries a battered briefcase.*)

PEGGY.   We have a guest! (*Turning on a light.*) This is Floyd, people. He's an Assistant Professor of Dramatic Literature, specializing in modern American drama.

25

FLOYD.   Eugene O'Neill through David Mamet, actually. Though I also do a broad survey of world theatre.

PEGGY.   Floyd, this is my husband Roger, a successful American businessman.

ROGER.   *(Shaking hands.)* Hello, Floyd.

PEGGY.   And this is Julia, who purports to be a friend of the family.

JULIA.   *(Shaking hands.)* Hello, Floyd. Do you have tenure?

FLOYD.   Not yet.

JULIA.   Thank God.

FLOYD.   Enough chit-chat, gang. Everybody please sit down. *(They all do, like students in a course.)* I suppose I should say at the start that you will be judged as much by your comments along the way as by what you may write on the exam.

ROGER.   Exam? Do you give exams?

FLOYD.   I do indeed. I think it's important to pull things together at the end. I normally ask people to write an essay of eight to ten pages.

ROGER.   Single or double spaced?

FLOYD.   Double. But in this case, we might settle for oral examinations.

JULIA.   *(Low to Roger.)* He sounds like a dentist.

FLOYD.   Who said that? *(Pause.)* I'm waiting. *(Pause.)* We will simply stand here, wasting valuable stage time, until the person who made that remark has the courage to admit it.

JULIA.   *(Finally.)* I said it.

FLOYD.   Why?

JULIA.   Because I thought it was funny.

FLOYD.   And was it?

JULIA.   It didn't get quite the laugh I thought it would.

FLOYD.   Exactly, Julia. And I'll tell you why. Because it wasn't serious. Comedy, people, is a serious business. And now we've learned that, let's move on. *(Peggy raises her hand.)* Yes, Peggy.

PEGGY.   I'm worried about something on the stove. May I be excused?

FLOYD.   You may.

PEGGY.   All of you should feel free to talk about me when

I'm gone. *(She goes.)*

FLOYD. *(Looking after her.)* Now that was a sweet exit! "Talk about me when I'm gone." I liked that remark. Of course most of theatre is about that.

JULIA. Most of life is about that.

FLOYD. Wrong. Another half-baked remark. Beware of comparing life and the theatre, gang. Life is sprawling and unpredictable. Theatre is confined and artificial. There is no comparison, unless your own life happens to be confined and artificial as well. Is it, Julia?

JULIA. Um ... ah ...

FLOYD. Well, we'll find out soon enough, won't we?... No, people, life is action, theatre is talk. Or rather, in the theatre, talk is action. In any case, the best theatre is primarily the best talk. Which is why I become immediately impatient ... *(Looking at Julia.)* with characters who talk before they think.

ROGER. *(Saving the day.)* Uh, could we talk about Peggy? Now she's gone?

FLOYD. Raise your hand please, Roger.

ROGER. *(Raising his hand.)* Did you have a chance to observe my wife?

FLOYD. I did.

ROGER. Do you have any thoughts, based on your observations?

FLOYD. I'd say she was a mighty attractive woman.

ROGER. Thanks. I agree.

JULIA. We think she's nuts. Do you?

FLOYD. Hand, please.

JULIA. Do you think she might have psychological difficulties?

FLOYD. Not necessarily. I'll simply say that she seems like a woman waiting.

ROGER. A woman waiting ...

FLOYD. Yes, she's waiting for something — some scene, some action, some plot — which will enable her to play a meaningful role. Out there, she was like an actress waiting to come on. In here, she was like an actress waiting to go off. Note now that she is preparing dinner. I suspect, when it is done, she will serve it to us — *wait* on us, so to speak. Waiting. Always waiting. I am reminded of Samuel Beckett.

ROGER.   Is that good?

FLOYD.   That is *very* good. My compliments to your wife, sir.

ROGER.   Thank you, Floyd.

JULIA.   But she hasn't got a plot!

FLOYD.   I'll bet you have a plot, don't you, Julia?

JULIA.   As a matter of fact, I do. Yes.

FLOYD.   I'll bet you do. And I'll bet it's one of those cheap second rate triangle things, leading from adultery to divorce.

JULIA.   At least it keeps things moving.

FLOYD.   Better Beckett than that.

JULIA.   Yes, well, we'll see.

FLOYD.   I hope we do, Julia. I hope your clichéd little plot collapses before the evening is half over.

JULIA.   I like to think —

ROGER.   Hey, guys. Jesus. We're getting all hung up on plot here. I'm worried about my WIFE!

FLOYD.   You're right, Roger. We've gotten ahead of ourselves. It's always better to begin by discussing the set. *(He looks around.)* So this is the sacred space, eh?

ROGER.   This is it.

FLOYD.   This is the grove of Dionysos.

ROGER.   I guess.

FLOYD.   *(Indicating.)* And this, I assume, is the infamous fourth wall.

ROGER.   Right.

JULIA.   Note how all the furniture faces it.

FLOYD.   I am familiar with the requirements of realistic drama, madam. You forget I teach the stuff.

JULIA.   *(Under her breath.)* Well hoity-toity to you.

FLOYD.   I'll consider that a "stage whisper," and ignore it. *(Poking around like a detective.)* Now. Yes. Hmmm. The set is pretty much as you described it, Roger. You did a fine job on the telephone, and if this were a course in the visual arts, I'd give you a straight A.

ROGER.   Thanks, Floyd.

FLOYD.   That's the good news. The bad news is it's ridiculously old fashioned. I am amazed, I am truly amazed, that in this day and age, someone would bother to design a set like this.

JULIA. I personally think, with the right adjustments, it could be a lovely room.

FLOYD. In 1925, perhaps. In 1938, at a stretch. Possibly in Britain, for a brief nostalgic period after World War II. *(He picks up the vase indicated earlier by Roger and looks at it.)* But not in America at the tail end of the 20th Century! *(He hurls the vase into the fireplace.)* No. I'm sorry, people. Bourgeois domestic comedy is dead! And I, for one, am glad to see it go! *(Roger and Julia jump up.)*

JULIA. That lovely little vase!

ROGER. *(Going to the fireplace.)* It symbolized our marriage! *(He picks up a shard, looks at it lovingly.)*

FLOYD. Consider it just a prop, Roger. *(He begins to mix himself a drink at the bar.)* Let it symbolize your last link to the past.

ROGER. Oh yeah? Well that liquor's a prop, too, Floyd! You're mixing yourself a glass of water!

FLOYD. I know that, Roger. But notice how well I'm doing it.... Now sit down, people. *(Roger and Julia uneasily resume their seats. Floyd continues to mix his elegant martini.)* Derivation of the word "prop": short for "stage property," people. Came into use in the Eighteenth Century. Think of it also as a support. It "props" you up. We academics are really actors, you know. We strut and fret our hour in front of the class, and we too need our props — a book, a piece of chalk, or in this case a drink — to lean on. They give us something to do. *(He finishes making his drink.)*

JULIA. You said earlier that this sort of play is dead.

FLOYD. I did. Yes, I did. Yes.

JULIA. If so, why are you bothering to stick around?

FLOYD. That's the first good question you've asked, Julia. And so I'll tell you. I am "sticking around" because there is one thing which intrigues me about this room.

ROGER. What thing?

FLOYD. This fourth wall.

ROGER.   This fourth wall?

FLOYD.   This, don't you see, redeems things. It's here, it dominates the room, and it implies a world beyond the world it is supposed to contain.

ROGER.   And you think that's good?

FLOYD.   I think it might be. Yes. You wonder if your wife is insane, Roger. My answer is possibly no. By insisting on this wall, she may be more in tune with the post-modern world than anyone else in this room — except myself. Simply through the configuration of this room, Roger, your wife may be subtly challenging western democratic capitalism at its very core.

ROGER.   Like Melville's *Bartleby*.

FLOYD.   Exactly, Roger! Very good! But she may be going farther. She may be saying that there is something more than material success and the quaint pleasures of hearth and home. At a time when communism has collapsed in ruins and the lowliest citizen of the poorest country secretly aspires to live in a room just like this, your wife may be saying: No, don't bother, it's not worth it, because there is a world elsewhere, a world beyond this wall, which is far more worth reaching for. It is a daring room, people, and therefore a dangerous one.

ROGER.   Dangerous? You mean my wife is in danger?

JULIA.   Nonsense. I noticed an excellent security system when I walked in the door.

FLOYD.   It will take more than a suburban burglar alarm to keep out the reactionary forces of militant capitalism, Julia.

ROGER.   Good lord.

FLOYD.   Now look, I could be all wrong on this thing. This could simply be another domestic comedy, the kind of thing which the English have always done better, and we Americans have vulgarized into the sit-com on TV. It could be that, and if it is, I swear I'll dismiss you both as soon as I finish my drink.

ROGER.   Or?

FLOYD.   Or ... it could be a deep and dangerous challenge to contemporary values, a major step into the twenty-first century, working *within* the rubrics of realistic drama yet systematically deconstructing them as it goes along.

ROGER.   How will you be able to tell?

FLOYD.   By talking to Peggy. Go get her immediately.

ROGER.   *(Hesitantly.)* I will. But ... *(Stops.)*

FLOYD.   But what?

ROGER.   I have to say, Floyd, I kind of hope this *is* just another conventional comedy. At least I hope it has a conventional happy ending. I mean, I really want my wife back.

FLOYD.   Oh come on, Roger. Join the modern world. Allow for some dissonance around here. Embrace the random. Who knows? I might even end up with her myself.

JULIA.   Yes, Roger. You heard him say how attractive she was.

FLOYD.   They call that a "plant" in the theatre. P-L-A-N-T. In the sense of a seed planted that will grow to fruition later on.

ROGER.   Well I don't like that plant, thanks.

JULIA.   Oh, Roger, grow up. Go with the flow. *(She takes his arm.)* Beside, you and I have our own little garden to cultivate, remember?

FLOYD.   Your task is simply to send in Peggy. What happens off-stage is no concern of mine.

JULIA.   Hear that, Roger? Come. Let's go. It's time to make our garden grow. *(She drags Roger off-stage. Floyd remains. He quickly thumbs through a magazine, then fusses with his hair. Then he moves to the piano. Slyly, he hits a key. Again the piano plays an introduction. He sings.)*

FLOYD.   *(Singing.)*
          "Why Shouldn't I
          Take a chance when romance passes by?
          Why shouldn't I know of love?
(He leans debonnairely on the piano.)
          Why wait around
          When each age has a sage who has found
          That upon this earth*

* See Special Note on Music on copyright page.

Love is all that is really worth
Thinking of ...
(He becomes more confident.)
It must be fun, lots of fun,
To be sure when day is done
That the hour is coming when
You'll be kissed and then you'll be kissed again."*
(Peggy enters, now wearing a kitchen apron, wiping her hands.)
PEGGY.   *(As the music continues under.)* You wanted to talk to me, Floyd?
FLOYD.   I did, Peggy. But first I wonder if you'd help me finish this song.
PEGGY.   Sure. Why not? *(Singing.)*
"All debutantes say it's good,
FLOYD.   *(Singing.)*
And ev'ry star out in far Hollywood
Seems to give it a try —
BOTH.   *(In harmony.)*
So why shouldn't I?"*
FLOYD.   Now sit down, Peggy.
PEGGY.   All right. *(She sits.)*
FLOYD.   If you don't mind, I'd like to switch from the lecture mode to the Socratic method, and ask you a series of pointed questions.
PEGGY.   Ask away.
FLOYD.   I hope you'll answer them as clearly and thoroughly as you can.
PEGGY.   I'll try.
FLOYD.   First: What are we having for dinner?
PEGGY.   Well I made this casserole. It's just chicken, and I threw in some cheese, and some left-over broccoli. And then I added —
FLOYD.   That's enough. It sounds good, and I think I'll stay.
PEGGY.   I'm glad I made enough.
FLOYD.   Now is it true, Peggy, that you think there are

* See Special Note on Music on copyright page.

32

people beyond that wall?

PEGGY.   *(Carefully.)* I think ... there could be. I think ... there should be.

FLOYD.   *Should* be, Peggy?

PEGGY.   I think it could be terrific if people could gather together somewhere, away from their CDs and TVs and VCRs, and see and hear live actors say serious things about what's going on in their city, in their country, and in their world.

FLOYD.   What you're saying is that any culture which cannot produce good theatre, and a good, solid audience to respond to it, is no culture at all.

PEGGY.   Maybe that's it.

FLOYD.   What you're also saying — now don't let me put words in your mouth, but what you *might* be saying is that most great Western nations — be it Greece in the age of Pericles or Elizabethan England — have produced great theatre when they were at their peak.

PEGGY.   Is that true?

FLOYD.   It is indeed. And maybe you're saying that we ourselves have had a whiff of that greatness even in this country, in the period from Eugene O'Neill through Arthur Miller, when indeed our country was at the height of its power.

PEGGY.   I ... could be saying that. Yes.

FLOYD.   And you're also saying that now that our theatre has declined, you're concerned that our greatness as a nation is declining as well. And therefore, this wall, and your yearning to reach beyond it, is an attempt to revitalize theatre in America and to keep our great country from sliding irrevocably into darkness and decay.

PEGGY.   That could be it!

FLOYD.   God, Peggy! You don't know how exciting this is! This afternoon, I was sitting alone in my office, hoping that one of my students in American Drama might stop by at least to chat. I knew this was unlikely, however, because this semester I am down to three students in that course: An ambitious young man who wants to write film scripts, a breathless young woman who once saw *Les Miserables,* and an exchange student from Bangladesh who signed up by mistake. Normally I would have used my spare time to prepare for next semester's course on World Drama, but I learned today that it's just been supplanted by a second section of a new course in "Media Studies" entitled *"The Brady Bunch* and Beyond."

PEGGY. You poor man.

FLOYD. No, no, not now! Because your husband called, and invited me here. And suddenly I find myself not simply *discussing,* but also actively *involved* in what could be a vital new American play! I mean, it's thrilling, Peggy! I feel we're on the brink of a major breakthrough! So I hope you'll forgive me if I ask a few more questions.

PEGGY. Shoot.

FLOYD. O.K. Here we go. Now. Let's suppose there are people there, Peggy, beyond that wall. You're here, and they're there, and suddenly here's your big moment: What would you do?

PEGGY. Um. Well. Hmmm. I think I'd make a speech.

FLOYD. All right, Peggy. And what would you say?

PEGGY. Can I talk about current issues?

FLOYD. You can do anything you want. This is your play, after all. You're the one who's hammering out a whole new form.

PEGGY. Then I'd say three things.

FLOYD. Just three?

PEGGY. Three, at the start.

FLOYD. O.K. Do it.

PEGGY. *(Gaining confidence.)* I'd start off easily. I'd use a simple example.

FLOYD. Example of what, Peggy?

PEGGY. Of how our country has gone off track. I'd talk about our obsession with Coca-Cola.

FLOYD. Coca-Cola?

PEGGY. And Pepsi, and all soft drinks, caffeinated or decaffeinated, carbonated or not. I'd say they're over-priced, and nutritionally useless, and terrible for your teeth. I'd say the amount of labor and money we spend producing, transporting, and consuming these useless beverages, and then dealing with their containers, is a total waste of time. I'd say we should all see to it that everyone in the world is able to drink and enjoy a free supply of cool, clear water.

FLOYD.   That's quite a statement, Peggy. That hits at the heart of a consumer society.

PEGGY.   But that's just the first thing I'd say.

FLOYD.   Just the first?

PEGGY.   The second would be to talk about Bill Clinton.

FLOYD.   You'd name him directly?

PEGGY.   Yes I would.

FLOYD.   So early in the game?

PEGGY.   I absolutely would. I'd say here is a man who, at the end of the century — at the end of the millennium! — now holds the most powerful position in the world! Here is a man who has been given the chance to clean up the mess we've made over the last forty years.

FLOYD.   Would you name names there as well?

PEGGY.   Of course I would. I'd bring up all those people who took their eyes off the road, and drove us into some ditch. I'd mention Johnson and Nixon and Reagan and Bush and —

FLOYD.   What would you say about Bush, for example?

PEGGY.   I'd say Bush had a special responsibility, because he grew up in a room just like this. But did he make any attempt to reach beyond that fourth wall? He did not. Which is why he's not President today.

FLOYD.   I'm not sure anyone in the theatre has pointed a finger so directly at a political figure since Aristophanes attacked the demagogue Cleon in his comic masterpiece, *The Birds*.

PEGGY.   Maybe, but I'd also say something about Cambodia.

FLOYD.   Cambodia?

PEGGY.   And Bosnia and the Sudan and anywhere else where people are in deep adversity. I'd say that the world is small enough now so that we can no longer ignore the suffering of our brothers and sisters in humanity, any more than we could ignore the suffering of our immediate family. I'd say we in this country have a human obligation to pull ourselves together, not simply so we can improve our own lives here, but rather so we can help suffering people elsewhere live any life at all.

FLOYD. You'd say all that?

PEGGY. I would! But you know what, Floyd? Anyone can stand around a room and make speeches. The important thing is to have them *connect*. With other people. And I have to say that more and more I feel that connection.

FLOYD. Through that fourth wall.

PEGGY. Through that fourth wall. *(A pause. Then.)*

FLOYD. Wait here a minute.

PEGGY. Where are you going?

FLOYD. To get the others.

PEGGY. Why?

FLOYD. I want to tell them that we have a plot.

PEGGY. We do?

FLOYD. We most certainly do! In fact, we have the plot of one of the great plays of this, or any other century! *(He starts out again.)*

PEGGY. Would you mind telling me what it is?

FLOYD. *(Coming back in.)* Oh. Sorry. I thought you knew: It's the plot of *Saint Joan*.

PEGGY. *Saint Joan?*

FLOYD. *Saint Joan!* I'm thinking particularly of the version by George Bernard Shaw.

PEGGY. I've never seen it.

FLOYD. It's about a young French peasant girl who tries to change the world.

PEGGY. That's hardly me. I'm not so young and I'm not a peasant. In fact, my grandmother was in the Social Register.

FLOYD. But you have a peasant innocence, Peggy, and a taste for natural fibers in your clothes.

PEGGY. That's true, I do.

FLOYD. Furthermore, like Joan, you seem to hear special

voices ...

PEGGY.   Beyond that fourth wall ...

FLOYD.   Beyond that fourth wall. And Joan acts on those voices. She goes to where the French Dauphin is huddling with his cronies, and persuades him to be the king he should be ...

PEGGY.   Just the way I'd go to Washington and get Bill Clinton to do the same ...

FLOYD.   That's it! Then Joan and the Dauphin win a series of battles against the English and try to kick them out of France.

PEGGY.   Just the way Bill and I will kick the lobbyists, and special interests, and all the other dead wood out of Washington!

FLOYD.   Precisely. And remember that Shaw's play is not just about a peculiar peasant girl and a few obscure battles during the Hundred Years War. What we are really seeing, Shaw tell us, is the rise of Protestantism and the birth of Nationalism.

PEGGY.   But how does that work with me?

FLOYD.   With you, in your attack on a consumer society, we're seeing the rise of what we might call Ecologism!

PEGGY.   I see.

FLOYD.   And in your concern to move beyond national boundaries, we have a new kind of *Post*-Nationalism, or better yet, *Trans*-Nationalism.

PEGGY.   O.K.

FLOYD.   But no matter what we name these things, you sense something outside yourself which is calling you to accomplish them — which means you're playing a new version of Joan of Arc.

PEGGY.   I guess I am.

FLOYD.   And that's what I have to go tell the others! *(He starts off.)*

PEGGY.   Wait! One more question!

FLOYD.   I have to say, Peggy, I'm becoming impatient with these delays. As a teacher, I'm eager to share my insights with others. As a lover of the theatre, I'm concerned that we're slowing down the action.

PEGGY. I just want to know one more little thing.

FLOYD. *(Impatiently; at doorway.)* And what's that?

PEGGY. What about the ending?

FLOYD. What about it?

PEGGY. Well, I mean, Saint Joan dies, doesn't she?

FLOYD. Of course she dies. She gets captured by the English and burned at the stake.

PEGGY. But —

FLOYD. Stop quibbling, Peggy! We're talking big time now! I wouldn't be surprised if we ended up in New York! Now I've GOT to go tell the others. *(He goes off. Peggy staggers back into the piano. It sounds a dissonant chord, then plays.)*

PEGGY. *(Singing.)*

> "Big Town, what's before me,
> Fair weather or stormy?
> Big Town, will I hit the heights
> And see my name in electric lights?
> Big Town, will I blunder,
> Fall down and go under
> Or will I rise and rise
> Till I scrape your skies?
> Big Town,
> Wise old town,
> What's the lowdown on me?"

(The telephone rings. She answers it.)

PEGGY. *(On telephone.)* Hello?... Yes, this is Peggy?... What? *(She faces front in shock and horror.)* Who is this? *(Then defiantly.)* I don't care what you do! I plan to follow this through to the end! *(She slams down the receiver, and starts to reprise the song proudly. Singing.)*

> "Big Town, what's before me,
> Fair weather or stormy?
> Big Town, will I hit the heights
> And see my name in —"*

* See Special Note on Music on copyright page.

(Floyd comes back in.)
FLOYD.   I have very bad news.
PEGGY.   So do I. *(They look at each other.)*

CURTAIN

ACT TWO

Floyd and Peggy stand in exactly the same positions as at the end of Act One.

PEGGY.   You said you had bad news.

FLOYD.   I did. And you said the same.

PEGGY.   Isn't it amazing how a sudden shock will affect our sense of time? I feel as if we'd been standing here, facing each other, for over fifteen minutes.

FLOYD.   Ditto. Well. You tell me your news, then I'll tell you mine.

PEGGY.   O.K. I just received a threatening phone call.

FLOYD.   Hmmmm. I thought things might get dangerous. Was it a man or a woman?

PEGGY.   Hard to tell. It was either a man who sings a decent tenor or a woman who smokes at least a pack a day. Either way, it was suggested in very sinister tones that I rearrange my furniture immediately.

FLOYD.   They don't like the Fourth Wall.

PEGGY.   They sure don't.

FLOYD.   I can pretty well guess who it was.

PEGGY.   You can?

FLOYD.   Sure. It's obviously one of three possibilities, in view of those speeches you made.

PEGGY.   Who, then?

FLOYD.   First, it might have been a critic, warning you about your attempt to move beyond realism.

PEGGY.   O.K. I can deal with that.

FLOYD.   Or else it might have been a spokesperson for the soft drink industry, angry at what you said about Coke.

PEGGY.   Well I'm sorry. I'd say it again.

FLOYD.   But frankly I think it's the third alternative.

PEGGY.   Who?

FLOYD.   Hillary Clinton.

PEGGY.   You mean, because of what I said about Bill.

FLOYD. No. Because she wants to play Saint Joan herself.

PEGGY. But it was a hoarse voice. Does she smoke?

FLOYD. I imagine secretly. I imagine she has to.

PEGGY. Well I'm sorry, but no matter who threatens me, these things should be said.

FLOYD. Then keep saying them, Peggy!

PEGGY. O.K. Now for your bad news.

FLOYD. I — I've decided not to tell you.

PEGGY. Hey! No fair!

FLOYD. I can't, Peggy, and here's why. You may have noticed that tonight we are caught in a death struggle between two sorts of plays.

PEGGY. Two sorts of plays?

FLOYD. One represents a uniquely American yearning for the democratic experience. The other is a cheap throw-back to the continental sex comedy.

PEGGY. I don't understand ...

FLOYD. I'm glad you don't. *(He looks off.)* But my job, as I see it, is to prevent the bad play from destroying the good. Which is why I won't sully this stage by telling you my news.

PEGGY. But does it have to do with my husband?

FLOYD. I'm not saying any more. As the watchman says in the *Agamemnon*, "an ox stands on my tongue."

PEGGY. *(Starting off.)* Then I'll see for myself.

FLOYD. *(Quickly.)* No don't. *(Pause.)* There's another reason why I don't want to tell you, Peggy.

PEGGY. Another reason?

FLOYD. I'm nervous that you'll blame the messenger. I'm frightened you'll confuse the teller with the tale. I'm not sure why, but I don't think I could stand that, Peggy.

PEGGY. I won't do it then.

FLOYD. Promise?

PEGGY. I swear.

FLOYD. All right. Then here goes.... You may remember I went off to tell Roger and Julia about the Saint Joan thing?

PEGGY. I remember very well. I thought you created a lot of suspense.

FLOYD. The suspense has evaporated, Peggy.

41

PEGGY. How come?

FLOYD. I couldn't tell them.

PEGGY. Why not?

FLOYD. They were ... unreceptive.

PEGGY. What do you mean?

FLOYD. They were in the bedroom. With the door locked.

PEGGY. What?

FLOYD. So I knocked. I even rattled the doorknob. Finally I put my ear to the door.

PEGGY. What did you hear?

FLOYD. Some of the most second-rate dialogue it has been my misfortune to listen to.

PEGGY. At least you heard dialogue.

FLOYD. I did. Then they opened the door.

PEGGY. Were their clothes in disarray?

FLOYD. Somewhat. And they behaved sheepishly.

PEGGY. Sheepishly?

FLOYD. They claimed they'd been watching television.

PEGGY. Do you believe that?

FLOYD. At least it explains the lousy dialogue. Television writing can be appalling.

PEGGY. Did you tell them about Saint Joan?

FLOYD. I tried. But they didn't listen.

PEGGY. Didn't listen?

FLOYD. They shushed me.

PEGGY. They SHUSHED you?

FLOYD. And waved me away.

PEGGY. Waved you AWAY?

FLOYD. And returned to the bed. Where they remained, sprawled on the bedspread, watching the tube.

PEGGY. No.

FLOYD. A sit-com, I might add.

PEGGY. No.

FLOYD. And a re-run at that.

PEGGY. Are you sure?

FLOYD. I am! — I mean the plot was vaguely familiar.

PEGGY. Oh God.

FLOYD. Exactly. "Oh God." Actually, the line from *Saint*

Joan is: "Oh God that madest this beautiful earth, when will it be ready to receive Thy saints?"

PEGGY.   Not by watching TV, I can tell you that.

FLOYD.   Of course not.

PEGGY.   This is horrible.

FLOYD.   You can see why I was a reluctant messenger.

PEGGY.   I should have known Julia would try to seduce Roger! It's been on her mind ever since she saw his underpants in third grade.

FLOYD.   And in their attempt to recapture these juvenile feelings, they've regressed to television.

PEGGY.   Which they're probably not even watching now. Which is probably just blabbing away in the background.

FLOYD.   I wouldn't be surprised.

PEGGY.   Oh Floyd.

FLOYD.   I'm sorry, Peggy. I really am.

PEGGY.   I wonder what Saint Joan would do about this.

FLOYD.   She'd ignore it. She'd have more on her mind than the backstage gropings of a couple of stock characters.

PEGGY.   That's true ...

FLOYD.   So don't let this throw a vulgar light on all we've accomplished so far.

PEGGY.   I'll try not to. *(A pause; they look off.)*

FLOYD.   *(Exploding.)* Television! I should have known! A major threat to the contemporary theatre! We could compete with the movies, but television!

PEGGY.   In our *bed*room! With another woman!

FLOYD.   Oh hell. Maybe our country deserves to decline. Rome had its bread and circuses. We have TV.

PEGGY.   *(Starting off.)* Not necessarily! I'm going to break up the party!

FLOYD.   *(Grabbing her arm.)* Wait!

PEGGY.   No! This time I'm off! They want sit-com, they'll get sit-com!

FLOYD.   *(Still holding her.)* Please, Peggy, stay just a little longer. I have one more thing to say.

PEGGY.   But it's time for me to act!

FLOYD.   Half of acting is listening, Peggy. I listened to your

43

speeches. Now you listen to mine.

PEGGY.   O.K. But if I lose concentration, I'm sure you'll know why. *(She sits reluctantly.)*

FLOYD.   *(Speaking with difficulty.)* Peggy, I want you to know that I have never, in all my years of teaching, made any kind of sexual advance toward any of my female students, no matter how attractive they may be.

PEGGY.   Good for you, Floyd.

FLOYD.   This is because I've always considered myself gay.

PEGGY.   You're sweet to tell me. Now can I go?

FLOYD.   No, listen. Please. There's something about this room which has reoriented me. As we've played our scenes together, Peggy, I've begun to have second thoughts about my sexuality. Even as I've announced the infidelity of your husband, I've had the strange yearning to take his place at your side.

PEGGY.   Floyd …

FLOYD.   No, really. In fact, I think I love you, Peggy. I want to be with you wherever you go. All right, I may be gay but why should that stop me? Gays on stage make spectacular lovers. English actors have been proving this for years. Well, they have the technique, but we have the feelings, Peggy. At least I have. For you. Tonight.

PEGGY.   Aren't you slipping into the continental sex comedy, Floyd?

FLOYD.   Maybe I am, but what the hell. Oh look, I don't have to sleep with you, though Lord knows I'd love to take a crack at it. I won't even play the frustrated lover, mooning at your side! May I simply hang out with you occasionally, screening your phone calls, opening your hate mail, maybe even sharing a pizza with you in lonely hotel rooms when you take this play on the road?

PEGGY.   But what about your teaching career? Don't you want tenure?

FLOYD.   *(Kneeling before her.)* How can I teach *Saint Joan* when I've met the real thing? *(Roger and Julia enter.)*

ROGER.   Are we interrupting something?

PEGGY.   *(Keeping Floyd on his knees.)* You certainly are.

ROGER.   We were watching TV.

PEGGY.   So I have heard.

ROGER.   No, darling, really. We were.

PEGGY.   With the door locked?

ROGER.   That was automatic, darling. A hangover from the days when the children used to barge in.

PEGGY.   Don't drag the children into this!

ROGER.   All right, darling. Here's the thing. Julia and I may have entered the bedroom with other intentions, but during the preliminaries I happened to roll onto the remote. The TV went on and naturally we watched it.

JULIA.   It just shows how television dominates our lives.

ROGER.   It turned out to be crummy. I was bored with it almost immediately.

PEGGY.   Oh yes? Then why did you continue to watch it?

ROGER.   I hoped it would get better.

FLOYD.   "Hoped it would get better, hoped it would get better." That's what they said about post-war Russian drama! *(The others look at each other, confused.)*

PEGGY.   And did it get better, Roger? After Floyd came and went?

FLOYD.   And left you to your own devices?

ROGER.   No it didn't, darling. It got worse.

JULIA.   I disagree completely. I thought it was getting quite good.

PEGGY.   Now I'm confused. Are we talking about sex or television?

FLOYD.   Only in America could such a question arise.

JULIA.   Well the answer is that he grabbed the remote and switched to the Sports Channel.

PEGGY.   This suddenly has the ring of truth. Men are always doing that. They remotely control almost every aspect of our lives, and we women have to accommodate ourselves passively to every channel they switch to.

ROGER.   Now hold on here! Just hold on! Who has accommodated himself to whom around here? Who's been putting up with this frigging fourth wall? Oh Peggy, I've loved you for a hell of a long time, but sometimes you're a royal pain in the ass! Now I'm telling you that nothing happened between Julia and me, and that's a hard thing to say because Julia is an extremely exciting woman!

JULIA.   Thank you, Roger.

ROGER.   And what if something *had*, Peggy? What if a guy happens to put his wee-wee into the wong woman — I mean, wrong woman? So the hell what? Maybe a man gets tired of the approved diet occasionally, and wants to bite into a good, unhealthy, sizzling steak?

JULIA.   Thank you, Roger.

ROGER.   I mean the French do it all the time. We're disappointed when they don't. Hindu Gods do it on temples. Hollywood stars do it on screen.

JULIA.   Folks in Siam do it. Look at Siamese twins.

ROGER.   And your buddy Bill Clinton did it!

PEGGY.   He did not!

ROGER.   I say he did! And Hillary welcomed him back, and the country elected him president!

JULIA.   That's why I voted for him.

FLOYD.   This scene will stand as the most insidious defense of adultery in all of western drama.

PEGGY.   *(Taking Floyd's arm.)* All right, Roger. Then may I do it, too?

ROGER.   No.

PEGGY.   Why not?

ROGER.   Because it would be completely out of character.

PEGGY.   My character has changed!

JULIA.   There. You see? As with most arguments between husbands and wives, you've both gotten absolutely nowhere.

PEGGY.   *(To Roger.)* Why don't you just go watch the Playboy Channel? That might solve everything.

ROGER.   I don't want to watch TV any more, Peggy. Ever. Except for the Buffalo Bills.

FLOYD.   Then welcome back to the living stage.

PEGGY.   No, Floyd. Wait. Not so fast, please. *(To Roger and Julia.)* First I have one final question to ask of Roger and Julia.

ROGER.   Shoot. I'm ready for it.

JULIA.   I have nothing to be ashamed of, at least this far in the plot.

PEGGY.   *(Carefully.)* Roger and Julia: When you were demonstrating your limited attention span in the bedroom, and Floyd and I were working through a very difficult scene here in the living room, did either of you give a thought to what might be happening in the kitchen?

ROGER.   The kitchen?

PEGGY.   Did either of you, for example, bother to look at what might be happening in the oven, or think about what we might do for a green vegetable, or check the freezer for any ideas on dessert? *(Roger and Julia look at each other guiltily.)*

ROGER.   I didn't.

JULIA.   Nor, I'm afraid, did I.

PEGGY.   I didn't think so. *(She starts off.)* Excuse me, Floyd. Apparently Saint Joan is still responsible for a meal.

ROGER.   Let me help you, sweetheart.

PEGGY.   No thanks. You'll just try to butter me up.

ROGER.   Let me at least wash the lettuce.

PEGGY.   All right. But no goosing or nuzzling or fooling around. I'm still very mad at you, Roger. You can't switch *my* channels so easily. *(She goes. He follows. Pause.)*

JULIA.   I'm hopeless in the kitchen. Being a New Yorker, I either order in, or eat out. *(No answer from Floyd.)* Even breakfast poses a problem. I don't understand stoves. I always burn my buns. *(Her little joke. Floyd opens a book, reads.)* Are you a good cook?

FLOYD.   *(Vaguely.)* Hmmm?

JULIA.   *(Shouting.)* I said are you a good cook?

FLOYD.   Umm-hmmm.

JULIA.   Really? Do you have any specialties?

FLOYD.   *(Vaguely; as he reads.)* Noisettes de veaux Angleterre ... gnocci e porcini di Firenze ... Trout Tel Aviv with Dead Sea dumplings ...

JULIA.   Yummy. Sounds delicious.... Maybe you'd cook for me sometime.

FLOYD.   No thanks. *(He closes his book, gets another, reads that.)*

JULIA.   Mind if I smoke?

FLOYD.   Yes.

JULIA.   You do? You really do?

FLOYD.   I really do.

JULIA.   Don't tell me you're one of those Health Nazis.

FLOYD.   I'm glad to say I am.

JULIA.   Then suppose I joined the Resistance and did it anyway?

FLOYD.   I wouldn't.

JULIA.   But I want to.

FLOYD.   There are no ashtrays here.

JULIA.   I'll use this little plate of Staffordshire china.

FLOYD.   I don't believe the good craftsmen in Staffordshire designed that plate as a receptacle for lipstick-stained butts.

JULIA.   Nonetheless, I think I'll employ it for such. *(She opens her purse, takes out a lovely cigarette case, a holder, and an expensive lighter.)*

FLOYD.   You might want to know that no one smokes on stage any more.

JULIA.   Oh really?

FLOYD.   It's a piece of stage business that's totally obsolete.

JULIA.   Then the theatre has lost another fine, old custom. If it's done well, it both looks seductive and reveals character. *(She takes a cigarette out of the case, taps it, puts it in the holder, and is about to light it.)* For example, watch how attractively I do this. You'll be reminded of the Lunts.

FLOYD.   If you light that butt, lady, I'll take it with all your other smoking paraphernalia, and shove it attractively up your twat. *(Long pause. Julia removes the cigarette from the holder, puts it back in the box, puts everything back in her purse, snapping each container closed with grim precision.)*

JULIA.   *(Finally.)* You're not very polite. You know that, I suppose.

FLOYD.   Yes. I know that.

JULIA.   I mean, all I'm trying to do is have a short scene with you, and you're making it virtually impossible.

FLOYD.   We don't belong in the same *play*, lady, much less the same scene.

JULIA.   And why, pray tell, do you say that?

FLOYD.   Because we've made a major breakthrough here today. We've opened the whole thing up. We've been talking about big issues here, and you're bringing it all back down to some second-rate, middle-class comedy of manners.

JULIA.   Oh really. And what "big issues" have you been talking about?

FLOYD.   Reforming this country, changing the world, all that.

JULIA.   Oh now come on.

FLOYD.   In fact, we've found certain strong parallels to Saint Joan.

JULIA.   *Saint Joan? (A tinkling laugh.)* Joan of Lorraine? The Arc family's little girl Joan? That Joan?

FLOYD.   That Joan.

JULIA.   *(More laughter.)* You must be kidding. *Saint Joan* as a subject in today's world? Why even the movie was a failure forty years ago! Grow up, Professor Loesser! Join the Twentieth Century!

FLOYD.   Yeah well, you might be interested to know that it's an eternal story. It stretches back to Antigone, and forward to *Thelma and Louise.*

JULIA.   Oh yes?

FLOYD.   Oh yes! And in all its many manifestations, there's no place in the cast for a type like you. So please find a reason to get off this stage, or I'll find one for you.

JULIA.   *(After a pause.)* Floyd.... May I call you Floyd?

FLOYD.   I don't give a shit.

JULIA.   Floyd, I have a friend ...

FLOYD.   I doubt that, Julia.

JULIA.   No, I do, Floyd. I have a friend who is a professional actress. She told me once that whenever she got into trouble in a scene, she tried to remember her original objective. Now what is *my* original objective? My original objective was simply to give an opinion of this wall.

FLOYD.   And? So?

JULIA.   But then, as things progressed, I revised that objective, Floyd. My objective became to seduce someone.

FLOYD. You mean Roger.

JULIA. I mean Roger. But recently, as you may have observed, Roger "passed," as they say in the theatre. Therefore, being a woman, I am capable of lowering my sights.

FLOYD. Don't get any ideas, lady.

JULIA. *(More tinkling laughter.)* What? You mean, you? With me? Oh heavens, no. What I meant was that I am modifying my objective once again. My objective is now simply and solely to engage you in casual conversation. All I want to do is keep the ball in the air and the air in the ball. That's my only objective at this point.

FLOYD. My objective remains what it has always been — to keep good theatre alive in this country, in order to create and maintain a healthy and self-critical society.

JULIA. But we'll *keep* theatre alive, dear heart, just by talking to each other.

FLOYD. Conversation is not dramatic dialogue.

JULIA. Oh come on. We've got to do *some*thing. I mean, here we are, in front of this stupid fourth wall. At least, tell me where you're from.

FLOYD. I'm not saying.

JULIA. Oh please. Just as an improvisation. Just to jump start us.

FLOYD. *(With a sigh.)* I happen to come from a very underestimated town.

JULIA. Name it, and we'll see.

FLOYD. I happen to come from right here.

JULIA. What? Buffalo? Beau Fleuve? Which is cruelly called The Mistake on the Lake?

FLOYD. This is my hometown.

JULIA. But I'm from Buffalo, too!

FLOYD. Come off it.

JULIA. I am. You would have known that if you had been here for the exposition.

FLOYD. I'm amazed.

JULIA. You see? You see where casual conversation can take us? Already we've struck a common chord. Shall we pursue the thread?

FLOYD. Oh hell, why not?

JULIA. Tell me about your family, for example.

FLOYD. You wouldn't know them.

JULIA. Oh please. I might.

FLOYD. I come from a very different world.

JULIA. But maybe your mother cleaned for us.

FLOYD. Actually, I have no family, Julia.

JULIA. Don't be silly. There must be more Loessers.

FLOYD. The name Loesser was given to me by my drama teacher in high school, who admired the composer of *Guys and Dolls*.

JULIA. But what was your surname before that?

FLOYD. I didn't have one. I was an orphan.

JULIA. An orphan?

FLOYD. When I was barely a few hours old, I was deposited on the steps of the Niagara Home for Little Wanderers by an unwed mother.

JULIA. No!

FLOYD. Yes. And I was raised there by a group of kindly social workers. No one ever adopted me because I had a slight bed-wetting problem, which now, goddammit, is virtually cured. *(Pause.)*

JULIA. You're not going to believe this, Floyd.

FLOYD. What?

JULIA. Well, here's the thing: I, yours truly, little old me, once had an illegitimate child.

FLOYD. You're kidding.

JULIA. No really. I did. I never thought I could talk about it, unless I was asked onto the *Oprah Winfrey Show*.

FLOYD. You? A mother?

JULIA. When I was very young. Before I became involved with Planned Parenthood.... And guess what I did with my illegitimate child.

FLOYD. I'd hate to think.

JULIA. I deposited it on the steps of the same institution which you referred to in your own narrative.

FLOYD. The Niagara Home for Little Wanderers?

JULIA.   The same.

FLOYD.   Fantastic.

JULIA.   I know it.

FLOYD.   Talk about coincidence.

JULIA.   Talk about plot.

FLOYD.   Small world, huh?

JULIA.   Old Home week.

FLOYD.   Niagara Home week.

JULIA.   Exactly! *(Both laugh.)* Now you see? You see what fun it can be when people just loosen up and converse?

FLOYD.   *(Putting aside his book.)* I do. I'm beginning to see that.

JULIA.   All right, now let's just keep going, shall we? Just to see where things lead?

FLOYD.   Oh hell. Sure. Why not?

JULIA.   All right. Now tell me, Floyd: How old are you, more or less? Just give me a ball park figure.

FLOYD.   I'll tell you this: Today's my birthday.

JULIA.   Well happy same!

FLOYD.   Thanks, Julia.

JULIA.   I should have a present or something. *(She looks around, then offers him a knickknack from a nearby table.)*

FLOYD.   Oh no, no, no.

JULIA.   Now wouldn't it be amusing if my lost child were approximately the same age?

FLOYD.   That would be a good one, wouldn't it!

JULIA.   Well now you wait. We can actually check.

FLOYD.   You can check?

JULIA.   Absolutely. I just happen to be wearing ... *(She takes a locket from around her neck.)* This locket, containing the date of birth and a scrap of the little nightgown the infant wore when I presented it to the orphanage. I wear this everywhere. Except on the subway, of course. *(She gets it out.)* There. See? The birth date? Read it, would you please? I don't have my glasses.

FLOYD.   *(Reading.)* It's today's date!

JULIA.   No!

FLOYD.   I swear!

JULIA. I just can't believe this! We're beginning to sound like Dickens! It must be this silly fourth wall!

FLOYD. *(Getting out his wallet.)* Actually, I always carry with me a scrap of the nightshirt I was found in.

JULIA. Wouldn't it be fun if they compared favorably?

FLOYD. That would be too much. *(Comparing the two pieces of cloth.)* Julia ...

JULIA. Now don't tell me.

FLOYD. No seriously. They compare! Look! They're virtually identical! And see? Only when you put them together, can you read the following message: "Tumble dry under moderate heat."

JULIA. I can't believe this!

FLOYD. I mean, Jesus, we were just talking, and out all this stuff comes. You were right, Julia, about the natural flow of conversation. It makes me think I've been much too structured, both in the classroom and outside.

JULIA. I'm very tempted to tell the others.

FLOYD. Think we should?

JULIA. They might get a kick out of it.

FLOYD. Maybe we ought to make a call first.

JULIA. A call?

FLOYD. To the Niagara Home for Little Wanderers. Just to make sure.

JULIA. You think so?

FLOYD. I've learned in academia never to leap to conclusions.

JULIA. I suppose you're right.

FLOYD. I mean, take the little nightshirts, for example. Lots of babies might have worn them.

JULIA. I suppose. The Fifties were conformist times.

FLOYD. *(Picking up the phone.)* May I have directory assistance, please?...

JULIA. Wait, Floyd, I noticed a telephone in the den. Maybe we should call from there. I mean this is a rather private issue.

FLOYD. *(Hanging up.)* You're right.

JULIA. *(Taking his arm.)* Let's go, then! I wonder if these orphanages give out information over the phone?

FLOYD.   They have to these days. It's the law. All you need is a valid credit card. *(They start out.)*

JULIA.   *(Stopping.)* Floyd …

FLOYD.   What?

JULIA.   In view of how far we've come, I wonder if now you might let me celebrate by smoking one little ciggy-poo?

FLOYD.   Only if you let me bum one.

JULIA.   Oh you! You are a piece of work, Floyd! You really are! *(They go off laughing. After a moment, Roger comes in, looks at the piano, moodily hits a key. It plays.)*

ROGER.   *(Singing.)*

> "After you, who
> Could supply my sky of blue?
> After you, who
> Could I love?
> After you, why
> Should I take the time to try
> For who else could qualify
> After you, who?
> Hold my hand and swear
> You'll never cease to care
> For without you there,
> What could I do?
> I could search years
> But who else could change my tears
> Into laughter after you."*

(The piano continues to play, as Roger looks off, longingly. He reprises the last part of the song D. As he finishes the song, Peggy comes in carrying two plates of food which she sets down on the coffee table in front of the couch.)

PEGGY.   Come eat.

ROGER.   Where are the others?

PEGGY.   Telephoning in the den. They said to go ahead.

ROGER.   I'll see how long they'll be.

PEGGY.   Roger …

* See Special Note on Music on copyright page.

ROGER.   What?

PEGGY.   I think we should have a scene together. By ourselves.

ROGER.   Couldn't we have it in the kitchen?

PEGGY.   It belongs here. In front of that wall.

ROGER.   But I love eating in the kitchen. Remember when the kids were still around? Eating in the kitchen and watching *Jeopardy?* I loved all that.

PEGGY.   See? There you are. Always falling back on the television. Now please. Sit down. *(He does.)*

ROGER.   Suddenly I feel very nervous.

PEGGY.   So do I. Maybe we're both subconsciously reminded of the final scene in *The Doll's House,* by Henrik Ibsen.

ROGER.   Uh-oh. We read that my freshman year in college.

PEGGY.   So did we. In those days, everyone seemed to read the same thing.

ROGER.   Would you refresh my memory on that final scene? I got a C in English because I spent too much time playing freshman lacrosse.

PEGGY.   I only got a B minus, but I think what happens is the wife sits her husband down and explains to him why she's leaving him.

ROGER.   Leaving?

PEGGY.   Walking out.

ROGER.   Forever?

PEGGY.   You have that feeling.

ROGER.   Why?

PEGGY.   Because he never took her seriously.

ROGER.   I've taken you seriously.

PEGGY.   As a wife, yes. As a mother, oh yes. But as *me,* as a person in my own right, never. When it comes to things that have nothing to do with our cozy little family, you've never really listened to what I had to say.

ROGER.   Peggy …

PEGGY.   No, I mean this now. If you and I had just sat down and had this scene at the beginning, we probably wouldn't be having it at all.

ROGER.   Your logic eludes me, darling.

PEGGY.   No it doesn't. You know exactly what I mean. You just don't want to deal with it.

ROGER.   Sweetheart ...

PEGGY.   You never do. We've been very lucky, you and I, Roger. With the kids, with your work, with everything. And that's made us smug and safe and selfish. I had to shake things up.

ROGER.   Consider me shook.

PEGGY.   I wonder. I try to open up our life, and what do you do? You bring in Julia to trivialize the problem, and then you bring in Floyd to categorize it academically.

ROGER.   Sweetheart ...

PEGGY.   And you think if everyone sings Cole Porter, it will solve everything.

ROGER.   I love Cole Porter.

PEGGY.   I know you do, darling, and so do I. But he's no solution for what ails us.

ROGER.   He's a serious guy, Peggy. There's an oh-such-a-hungry-yearning burning inside of him.

PEGGY.   I'm not going to argue about the score, Roger. There's a certain inevitability in plays. And a certain progression in the history of modern drama. I also learned that in freshman English. After Ibsen comes Shaw. Which means that after we do *The Doll's House*, I've got to go off and play Saint Joan.

ROGER.   Are you going to put on armor, or can you play it in pantyhose?

PEGGY.   Goddammit Roger, I've just discovered a fifth wall here tonight.

ROGER.   Oh no! Not a fifth! Please! I can't even handle the fourth.

PEGGY.   Well when you do, there's still a fifth to get through. And that's the wall between men and women. Which may be the toughest of all to crack. Now good-bye. I'm on my way to Washington.

ROGER.   Washington? Floyd mentioned New York.

PEGGY.   I've decided Washington.

ROGER.   That's a dangerous town, love.

PEGGY.   I'll change that. I plan to put a fourth wall in the White House.

ROGER.   That may not be feasible, Peggy. It's an oval office.

PEGGY.   Still I'll do it. Then I'll put one in every house in America.

ROGER.   Lots of people don't have one wall these days, darling, much less four.

PEGGY.   All the more reason to get going.

ROGER.   Why you, darling?

PEGGY.   Because I want to. Because I said I would. Because people are counting on me.

ROGER.   What people?

PEGGY.   Those people! Beyond the wall! Oh Roger, where the hell have you been?

ROGER.   I've been here, love. All evening. And I have to tell you, in all honesty, I don't think there's anyone there.

PEGGY.   You don't?

ROGER.   I don't. That wall just holds up our house. Period.

PEGGY.   That's all?

ROGER.   And that's enough. And even supposing there *were* people beyond it, Peg, I don't think they'd expect you to change the world. Maybe they'd be amused. Maybe even interested. But in the end, they wouldn't take this Saint Joan thing terribly seriously.

PEGGY.   You don't think so?

ROGER.   I really don't, sweetheart. Plays never change the world, Peg. And the ones that try are the ones that never last.

PEGGY.   *(Sitting down.)* Oh boy.

ROGER.   *(Sitting beside her; putting his arm around her.)* Oh sweetheart, look. We've had a good time here tonight. We've had a laugh or two. You've said some things that ought to be said. But now don't you think it's time we put the furniture back the way it was?

PEGGY.   The way it was?

ROGER.   I promise I'll turn off the TV and talk eyeball to eyeball with you any time you want!

PEGGY.   You mean you want to just sit around and grow old?

ROGER.   *(Putting his arm around her.)* And enjoy each other. And our friends. And our kids. And maybe grandchildren some day. Leave politics to the politicians. Let's hunker down at home.

PEGGY.   So what you're saying is I've run up against a blank wall.

ROGER.   That's what I'm saying, darling.

PEGGY.   Like Melville's *Bartleby?*

ROGER.   Like Melville's *Bartleby. (Julia and Floyd come in.)*

JULIA.   *(Seeing them together on the couch.)* You look so gloomy. Has somebody died?

PEGGY.   Only a dream.

JULIA.   Well I want to thank you for the use of your telephone.

ROGER.   I hope it served its purpose.

FLOYD.   It did and it didn't.

ROGER.   Meaning?

FLOYD.   We thought we'd have a surprise for both of you.

JULIA.   We thought we'd discovered we were related.

FLOYD.   In fact, I secretly hoped we'd be able to dramatize the connectedness of all human beings.

PEGGY.   Oh that would have been wonderful!

FLOYD.   But this was not to be.

JULIA.   It turns out that the illegitimate child I deposited at an orphanage years ago was female, rather than male. It simply slipped my mind.

FLOYD.   The child was obviously not me, and I'd be glad to prove it.

JULIA.   *(To Floyd.)* That won't be necessary, dear. *(To others.)* In my eagerness to carry on a conversation, I assumed too much.

FLOYD.   And in my eagerness for a recognition scene I went along with it. Art is not life, people. And what happens on stage tends to be modified once we're in the wings.

JULIA.   *(Taking Floyd's arm.)* On the other hand, we've

been on a meaningful journey together, and have formed a friendship with no sexual component whatsoever. This is new to me, of course. You might say I have broken through my own personal fourth wall.

FLOYD.   And as for me, I feel that life has at last penetrated the academic shell I've built around myself. Next semester, I plan to take a sabbatical from teaching, and concentrate simply and solely on my bedwetting problem.

JULIA.   I'll help you, dear.

FLOYD.   I'd appreciate that.

ROGER.   Then here's what we do. *(He goes to the piano, hits a note. The piano plays an introduction.)*

PEGGY.   Knew it. He's trying to end this thing with Cole Porter.

ROGER.   *(Singing.)*

"What say? Let's be buddies,

What say? Let's be pals ...

(Julia joins him.)

JULIA.   *(Singing.)*

What say? Let's be buddies,

And keep up each other's morals.

(Floyd joins them.)

FLOYD.

I may never shout it,

But many's the time I'm blue ...."

ROGER.   Come on, Peg ...

(Peggy joins them reluctantly.)

ALL.   *(In good harmony.)*

"What say? How's about it?

Can't I be a buddy with you?"

ROGER.   O.K. Once again, now. From the top ...

ALL.   *(Singing.)*

"What say, let's be buddies ...

JULIA.   *(Improvising.)*

Bosom buddies ...*

* See Special Note on Music on copyright page.

ALL.

> What say, let's be pals ...

ROGER.   *(Improvising.)*

> Like Hope and Crosby ...

ALL.

> What say, let's be buddies ...

FLOYD.   *(Improvising.)*

> Like Beaumont and Fletcher!

ALL.

> And keep up each other's morals ..."

ROGER.   *(Spoken.)* Take it, Peg!

PEGGY.   *(Singing.)*

> "I may never shout it ..."*

(Suddenly breaking away from the group.) I can't do this. *(The piano dies out.)*

ROGER.   Why not? You were doing fine.

PEGGY.   That's just it. It reminds me how great it is when people get together and sing.

JULIA.   Only in small groups, darling. When they're old friends. And know the words.

PEGGY.   But I want other people to get it on it. I want everyone in the world to be singing different parts to some basic underlying melody.

JULIA.   *(To Floyd.)* Is she talking about opera?

FLOYD.   No, she's talking about the social contract, as proposed by Jean-Jacques Rousseau in the Eighteenth Century.

PEGGY.   Whatever it is, I've got to get people to do it. *(She starts out.)*

ROGER.   Not everyone can carry a tune, Peg.

PEGGY.   Then they can beat the drum. Come on, Floyd. Time to march into battle.

FLOYD.   March? I'm just learning how to walk, Peggy.

PEGGY.   O.K. Then I'll go alone.

ROGER.   No, wait. What about the exam? Early in the evening, Floyd mentioned an exam.

---

* See Special Note on Music on copyright page.

JULIA. Yes. That was a plant, Peggy. You just can't leave it hanging there.

ROGER. Right. You've got to take the exam, Peg.

FLOYD. She's already passed. Summa Cum Laude.

PEGGY. Thank you, Floyd. *(She kisses him on the cheek.)* And thanks for my plot.... Good-bye, Julia. *(Kisses Julia, remembers both cheeks; turns to Roger, gives him a warm kiss.)* Good-bye, darling. I'll miss you. Now there are lots of leftovers in the freezer. They'll last till you learn how to cook.

ROGER. I won't bother! I'll eat Chinese! I'll have an affair!

JULIA. *(Taking Floyd's arm.)* Not with me, please. I'm over all that.

ROGER. *(Blocking the doorway.)* I won't let you go, Peggy! I'll keep you here by force!

PEGGY. *(Touching his lips.)* Don't be silly, darling. Good-bye. *(She exits blithely through the fourth wall, is hit by a lovely light. She sees the audience.)* I KNEW it! I knew you'd be there! Oh I wish we could all get together, but first I've got to go to Washington and change the world!... *(She greets people as she goes up the aisle.)* Good-bye.... Good-bye.... Anything you want me to tell Bill?... Wish me luck.... Good-bye! *(She exits through the audience. Pause.)*

FLOYD. Wow! Did you see that? She broke the proscenium!

JULIA. She must have done it with mirrors.

ROGER. Quickly, Floyd. Was Saint Joan married?

FLOYD. Of course not.

ROGER. She must have had lovers.

FLOYD. Only in Schiller and Verdi.

ROGER. Shit! I can't speak German or Italian!

FLOYD. In Shaw, there's a loyal soldier who follows her around. I wanted to play it once upon a time.

ROGER. I could do that.

FLOYD. It's kind of a minor role.

ROGER. Maybe I've played the lead too long. *(He hesitates, then closes his eyes, and steps through the wall; again a new light hits him. He sees the audience.)* Well, what d'you know? She was right! *(Calls after Peggy.)* Wait, darling! Wait! I'm coming, too!

(He greets people as he hurries up the aisle.) Hello.... Hello.... Peg! I've got the credit cards! *(He exits through the audience. Pause.)*

JULIA. *(Looking out blankly.)* Hmmm. *(Pause; then shrugging it off.)* Oh well. That's the end of a rather pleasant little evening.

FLOYD. *(Looking at the wall.)* As Shaw says at the end of *Saint Joan,* I wonder ... *(The piano sounds a note. They look at each other.)*

JULIA. *(Singing.)*
    "Can't I be a buddy?

FLOYD. *(Singing.)*
    Can't I be a buddy?

BOTH. Can't I be a buddy to you?"* *(They embrace.)*

CURTAIN

* See Special Note on Music on copyright page.

PROPERTY LIST

China plate
3 magazines
Vase
2 champagne flutes
Rock glass
Cocktail napkins
Stirrer
Ice bucket with ice
Champagne bucket with champagne bottle
Bar towel
Dry vermouth bottle
Tanqueray bottle
Purse (JULIA) with:
    cigarette case with cigarettes
    cigarette holder
    cigarette lighter
Briefcase (FLOYD) with:
    5 books
    folders
    notes
    index cards
Apron (PEGGY)
2 plates with food (PEGGY)
2 napkins (PEGGY)
2 forks (PEGGY)
Pen (FLOYD)
Locket and chain (JULIA)
Wallet with fabric scrap (FLOYD)

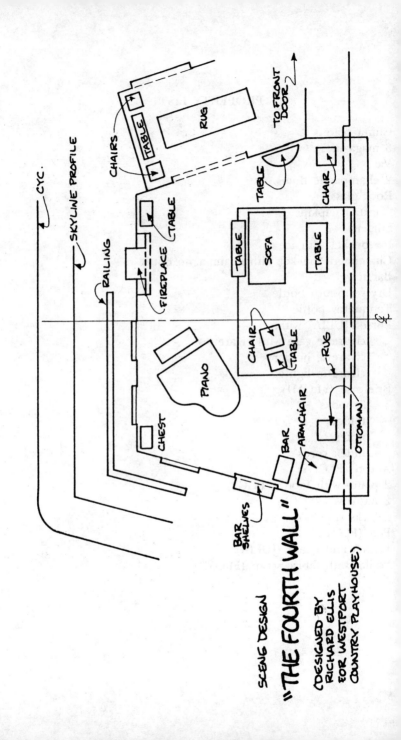

SCENE DESIGN

"THE FOURTH WALL"

(DESIGNED BY
RICHARD ELLIS
FOR WESTPORT
COUNTRY PLAYHOUSE)

TODAY'S HOTTEST NEW PLAYS

❏ **MOLLY SWEENEY by Brian Friel, Tony Award-Winning Author of** *Dancing at Lughnasa.* Told in the form of monologues by three related characters, *Molly Sweeney* is mellifluous, Irish storytelling at its dramatic best. Blind since birth, Molly recounts the effects of an eye operation that was intended to restore her sight but which has unexpected and tragic consequences. *"Brian Friel has been recognized as Ireland's greatest living playwright. Molly Sweeney confirms that Mr. Friel still writes like a dream. Rich with rapturous poetry and the music of rising and falling emotions...Rarely has Mr. Friel written with such intoxicating specificity about scents, colors and contours." - New York Times.* [2M, 1W]

❏ **SWINGING ON A STAR (The Johnny Burke Musical) by Michael Leeds. 1996 Tony Award Nominee for Best Musical.** The fabulous songs of Johnny Burke are perfectly represented here in a series of scenes jumping from a 1920s Chicago speakeasy to a World War II USO Show and on through the romantic high jinks of the Bob Hope/Bing Crosby "Road Movies." Musical numbers include such favorites as "Pennies from Heaven," "Misty," "Ain't It a Shame About Mame," "Like Someone in Love," and, of course, the Academy Award winning title song, "Swinging on a Star." *"A WINNER. YOU'LL HAVE A BALL!" - New York Post. "A dazzling, toe-tapping, finger-snapping delight!" - ABC Radio Network. "Johnny Burke wrote his songs with moonbeams!" - New York Times.* [3M, 4W]

❏ **THE MONOGAMIST by Christopher Kyle.** Infidelity and mid-life anxiety force a forty-something poet to reevaluate his 60s values in a late 80s world. *"THE BEST COMEDY OF THE SEASON. Trenchant, dark and jagged. Newcomer Christopher Kyle is a playwright whose social satire comes with a nasty, ripping edge - Molière by way of Joe Orton." - Variety. "By far the most stimulating playwright I've encountered in many a buffaloed moon." - New York Magazine. "Smart, funny, articulate and wisely touched with rue...the script radiates a bright, bold energy." - The Village Voice.* [2M, 3W]

❏ **DURANG/DURANG by Christopher Durang.** These cutting parodies of *The Glass Menagerie* and *A Lie of the Mind,* along with the other short plays in the collection, prove once and for all that Christopher Durang is our theater's unequivocal master of outrageous comedy. *"The fine art of parody has returned to theater in a production you can sink your teeth and mind into, while also laughing like an idiot." - New York Times. "If you need a break from serious drama, the place to go is Christopher Durang's silly, funny, over-the-top sketches." - TheatreWeek.* [3M, 4W, flexible casting]

DRAMATISTS PLAY SERVICE, INC.
440 Park Avenue South, New York, New York 10016 212-683-8960 Fax 212-213-1539

TODAY'S HOTTEST NEW PLAYS

❏ **THREE VIEWINGS by Jeffrey Hatcher.** Three comic-dramatic monologues, set in a midwestern funeral parlor, interweave as they explore the ways we grieve, remember, and move on. *"Finally, what we have been waiting for: a new, true, idiosyncratic voice in the theater. And don't tell me you hate monologues; you can't hate them more than I do. But these are much more: windows into the deep of each speaker's fascinating, paradoxical, unique soul, and windows out into a gallery of surrounding people, into hilarious and horrific coincidences and conjunctions, into the whole dirty but irresistible business of living in this damnable but spellbinding place we presume to call the world."* - New York Magazine. [1M, 2W]

❏ **HAVING OUR SAY by Emily Mann.** The Delany Sisters' Bestselling Memoir is now one of Broadway's Best-Loved Plays! Having lived over one hundred years apiece, Bessie and Sadie Delany have plenty to say, and their story is not simply African-American history or women's history...it is our history as a nation. *"The most provocative and entertaining family play to reach Broadway in a long time."* - New York Times. *"Fascinating, marvelous, moving and forceful."* - Associated Press. [2W]

❏ **THE YOUNG MAN FROM ATLANTA Winner of the 1995 Pulitzer Prize. by Horton Foote.** An older couple attempts to recover from the suicide death of their only son, but the menacing truth of why he died, and what a certain Young Man from Atlanta had to do with it, keeps them from the peace they so desperately need. *"Foote ladles on character and period nuances with a density unparalleled in any living playwright."* - NY Newsday. [5M, 4W]

❏ **SIMPATICO by Sam Shepard.** Years ago, two men organized a horse racing scam. Now, years later, the plot backfires against the ringleader when his partner decides to come out of hiding. *"Mr. Shepard writing at his distinctive, savage best."* - New York Times. [3M, 3W]

❏ **MOONLIGHT by Harold Pinter.** The love-hate relationship between a dying man and his family is the subject of Harold Pinter's first full-length play since *Betrayal*. *"Pinter works the language as a master pianist works the keyboard."* - New York Post. [4M, 2W, 1G]

❏ **SYLVIA by A.R. Gurney.** This romantic comedy, the funniest to come along in years, tells the story of a twenty-two year old marriage on the rocks, and of Sylvia, the dog who turns it all around. *"A delicious and dizzy new comedy."* - New York Times. *"FETCHING! I hope it runs longer than Cats!"* - New York Daily News. [2M, 2W]

DRAMATISTS PLAY SERVICE, INC.
440 Park Avenue South, New York, New York 10016 212-683-8960 Fax 212-213-1539